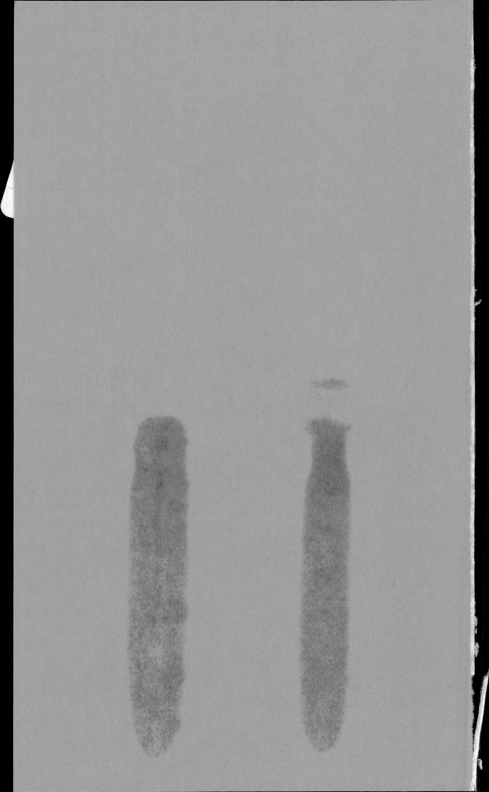

Dowry

Dowry

Poems by

Janet Beeler

A Breakthrough Book
University of Missouri
Columbia & London, 1978

cop. a

University of Missouri Press, Columbia, Missouri 65211
Library of Congress Catalog Card Number 77–18232
Printed and bound in the United States of America

Library of Congress Cataloging in Publication Data

Beeler, Janet.
  Dowry.

  (A Breakthrough book)
  I. Title.
PS3552.E345D6   811'.5'4   77–18232
ISBN 0–8262–0246–2

Acknowledgment is made to the following publications for poems that originally appeared:

The American Poetry Review: "Excavation at Mesa Verde," "Self," "The Sacrament of Penance," "Christine de Pisan," "Archeologist," "Muse," "Chinese Burial Cloth, Second Century." *Antaeus*: "Feeding Time," "How to Walk on Water," "The Animal Ship." *Best Poems of 1973* (Borestone Mountain Poetry Awards series): "Feeding Time." *Best Poems of 1975* (Borestone series): "Considerations on Indo-European Culture." *Cardinal*: "Probably." *Esquire*: "Bone Structure," "Cave," "Wedding Night: Chagall," "Waiting Room." *New Orleans Review*: "The Poetess Li Chi'ng Chao," "The Hired Mourner," "Metchilde," "Burial Day." *New Catholic World*: "Hand-Blown Glass," "Anniversary." *Open Places*: "Ice Fishing After," "Breaking Out," "The Liberian Whore," "Loving the White Bull." *Perspective*: "See the Artist at Work, 25¢," "Wake," "Considerations on Indo-European Culture." *Poet Lore*: "Passage," "The Lovers." *Primavera*: "Gaspara Stampa," "Mrs. Nakamura." *Rhino*: "Drawing Up."

For Bob

The Devins Award for Poetry

Dowry is the 1978 winner of The Devins Award for Poetry, an annual award originally made possible by the generosity of Dr. and Mrs. Edward A. Devins of Kansas City, Missouri. Dr. Devins was President of the Kansas City Jewish Community Center and a patron of the Center's American Poets Series. Upon the death of Dr. Edward Devins in 1974, his son, Dr. George Devins, acted to continue the Award.

Nomination for the Award is made by the University of Missouri Press from those poetry manuscripts selected by the Press for publication in a given year.

Contents

Part Two: Holy Women

Part One: Dowry

"To be loved means to be consumed.
To love is to give light with inexhaustible oil."

(written on the margin of the MS
of *The Notebooks of
Malte Laurids Brigge,* Rainer Maria Rilke)

Bone Structure

My hands, nails frail as isinglass
narrow bones, pale moons rising

steady enough to trim hair
from my father's nostrils and ears

last joint of one finger missing
rim of skin left, smooth as a circumcision

one ring a tarnished Indian band
green turquoise in silver, sand-cast

purchased for me out of pawn
by my husband, collector of vagrant forms

another ring, demanding only this man
and no other, only his children

I wear away at that gold shape
as a poet chafes the form he needs and hates

Feeding Time

Dusk again at the Old Forge dump.
Black heads honed with hunger
peer through the closing green,
then the bears emerge
furred in pitch shadows.

In this green light they seem to float,
graceful as whales,
paddling at boxes of fish heads,
diving under crates of cabbage leaves,
their kitchen submerged in mist
and sinking deeper into the night stream.

My flashlight fixes two cubs in a fresh pit,
sucking on cider jugs
until their mother knocks them tumbling
to a treasure of beef bones
already sticking white as fingers
pointing from her teeth.

Grey muzzle, scarred hide,
fruit peel silver in his mouth,
only the oldest bear regards me.
He is the one I come to see,
and he drifts closer every night,
stiff-jointed,
his fur shined with slobber.
His flat black eyes
cleave to me as he eats.

After all these nights of watching
I have a place now in his hunger.

But what place has he in mine,
this great grey bear
stinking of fish and mud,
this enormous longing feeding on my dreams
each night?

How to Walk on Water

First test the surface with your palm.
It must be taut and pliant, moist
as the membrane inside your lips.

Wind can crumple the lake skin into tissue,
rain can thicken the transparent film
into green apple peel.

Walk only in the still of early morning
when the gloss of faint blue
is tense and unbroken.

Lift with your indrawn breath,
unreel your spine like a dancer rising
to make strength weightless.

Walk slowly. Some care must be taken.
Under, stones pulse like clams,
twigs wring shapes from themselves.

Your shadow slips away from you
entwining with other shadows,
as silver supple as a fish.

Your face reflects as an astonished moon.
Like the saints, you were afraid
in spite of the assurances.

But you are safe, walking on water,
unless you slit the surface carelessly
and plunge through the brown wound.

Once I even lay myself full length,
fifteen feet from shore, spread eagle
on the cool blue sheet.

Everything moved below, becoming—
a damselfly wing making the slow journey
back into stone,

shells already softening into moss,
bones emerging whiter now as reeds,
crayfish clarifying into mica.

Dowry

The pelt of old snow still stays
on the field,
a tattered sheepskin,
but there's a thin stain of sun.

Time to take out
these lengths of cloth
I wove in the dark seasons,
time to bring kettles to the barnlot
and boil my dyes—
yellowweed,
red from madder root,
woodwaxen as green as winter wheat,
the orange of bittersweet.

I'll stretch these new colors
up to dry on the frames you've made,
a bride making her first bed.
Barefoot, we'll strip off our winter clothes
and wash each other free
in this bright thaw.
Then wrap up in our dazzling sheets.

Your name like chrism on my lips,
let clear light rise in me.

See the Artist at Work, 25¢

spreads her canvas on the floor
sized, her own new ground
with no one pissing on the perimeters

lays out a full palette
asks the crowd to step back

takes off her clothes, her shoes
her religious medals
climbs to the back of the chair
leaps
artist and air shimmering over canvas
like heat over the Mojave

she ascends slowly
jackknifes
enters the paint first
toes pointed
no splash, strictly pro

drenched in color she bounces back
into an Immelman
descends to brush the canvas first
with her burnt sienna tongue
to rub her acra red face into the fibre

next, the sequence for which she will become
justly famous
series of half-gainers
contacts with mars black palms
unbleached titanium hair
one breast, her best one, cadmium orange
cerulean blue belly and both thighs

then quickly over onto her yellow hip
in ecstatic parabola

finally she dives under the buoyant new skin
made pliant with polymers
wraps it around
tucks in both feet
eases down into its tender umber
and smiling, falls asleep

Cave

Reach into this narrow mouth
with both hands.
Though limestone will not stretch,
the stone throat opens
to one who will go in alone.

Lay your cheek on black chill.
Now the mountain rests on your shoulder,
its breath cold as the breath of water.

Work through this granite wound.
Hands root ahead, eyeless,
seize the channel rim.
Push through,
though there are no hands
to catch this coming
into the cave.

After the first turn it is wholly night.
Your light finds boulders broken open,
calcite curves various as flesh,
rooms once boiled from rock,
glass veils,
fractures clotted with quartz.

Search the caverns.
Is he here, the white bull
born of the old gods,
who was calved here and returned
to die?
Touch the silence of his dark bones

before ascending to cicadas
and blind noon.

Excavation at Mesa Verde

He lay on his right side all his life.
His skull is flattened.

Steps are carved to his cave in the cliff.
There is a bowl by him for corn meal,
a gourd for water.

In his basket are bird bones,
his baby teeth,
smooth white stones like little eggs.

Through the cave opening
he could have seen the plain stretching
like a brown dog,
wild mustard,
the stream bed's snake tangle,
night coming on.

In the space between the child
and the high cave door
the woman's bones nest like a fence.

Wedding Night: Chagall

We float outside the windows,
body banners,
a trailing embrace refracting light,
becoming long blue dog,
long red cat entwined.

I have yellow Etruscan eyes,
a slender, tufted tail,
and claws caught in your fur.

You have arms like scarves,
wrapping my throat and waist,
and a bristly dog face,
black mouth, rough tongue
that blurs the outlines of my body
in our drunken comet kiss.

Bride and beast, beast and groom,
arching over house tops,
reeling with illusion
and the reality of the silky undercoat,
our constellation of desire
wheeling round toward home
as surely as Antares rising over us
in the clear, green sky.

Self

I roll my blouse sleeve up
clear to my armpit
and plunge my hand again
into the chill, dead water
in the rain barrel.

Leaves are clotted
in the cracks of the oak ribs,
and fresh leaves float a bracelet,
ascending my arm
with a pearly clasp
of insect spray and oil curds.

My breasts flatten out
against the iron rim
as I reach down and down.

Stretching, I can barely touch
the stripped fingers of twigs,
scraps of bark as supple as skin,
a naked maidenhair of moss,
vines in a knot of veins,
something like the pulp of fruit
in this abandoned barrel.

There. Behind the milk bottle.
Cushioned on its bed of silt
and silky mud,
it is hidden here
out of reach to all others.

It gives off no glint
through the dark water
but dense and heavy in my hand,
it lets me gauge
its shape and weight.

Hand-Blown Glass

First the fire
orange-hot, blue-hot
whimpering with flame
the ball is taken on the pipe

bend down to blow
a wind player playing glass
making no sound grow
round and rounder

dense form
shaped with breath
reshaped with wet wood
the globe thins and glows
as its shape blends with air
with mouths
with all openings made for shaping

clasped to another heat
curved with the hose
thinned, thinned
expanded in glass skin
sheer fruit
plunged into powdered shading
and picked
shimmering with peacock chemicals

cracked alone from the pipe
it gives off waves
of lessening light

last, in the cooling box
that narrow home
where heat is eased out
leaving form

Chorale

I see her running against the sky
through wild mustard and onion grass,
turning in the blue poise of evening,

as she hurls down to the chalked edge
of the cliff and without even slowing
leaps onto the shivering air.

Her long arc flares in the last sun,
then her russet shadow sailing down
embraces her self in the waves.

Later the boys appear, dreaming
her green going down before,
throwing off shirts and shoes

and carving slow white dives
slicing into wide reflected sky-
cries I cannot understand.

She rides their naked backs,
a sea turtle splitting crests,
a porpoise trailing the thin moon

in lazy tales spun out behind,
salt steaming on their skin,
water streaming between their teeth.

Again and again her first leaping forth,
sometimes her straw hat flung out,
sometimes cotton stockings like feathers

following her angle as she breaks
through the thin surface of flight,
and I watch from another shore.

Passage

He turned his head
meaning to ask the time, or call
for the pan on his bed,
or beg for more Demoral, (yes,
certainly for dope, he had been
coughing up
shreds of his lungs into paper cups
for six months by then).
He said nothing, instead;
she had already dissolved into darkness.

He still heard the tractor, the cat
purring under the bed.
Ted! she cried, and he heard that
last, wondering who is Ted?

Ice Fishing After

When she shattered,
milk broke,
honey froze
and splintered like cracked amber.

The stiff floe
pressed over pulse
until her throb stopped,
except for the current
deep in my breath.

Drill a hole,
build a hut and a pine fire,
squat inside and listen.

Beneath, a fish bedded in reeds,
blood shut down by ice,
drifts through its winter blindness
but casts no shadow
for my line to catch.

Dreamless swimmer,
learning the sleep of dark water,
is there one word left in the cold silt,
waiting to quicken?

Burial Day

on the way home
we stop at her picking garden
gone wild since July

tomato vines exploding fruit like nebulae
red suns, green moons

furry leaves parting
handfulls of little gold tomatoes
double handfulls of beefsteak tomatoes

her whole field for our feasting
spouts of hot juice in our mouths
juice on our chins
seeds and juice on our clothes

eating her tomatoes the way she liked to
warm in the field
without washing

without salt

For the Other Son

Daily I create myself:
cold water to waken,
a film of beige
and a thumb of rouge,
a streak of lavender
in the crease above the eyelid,
a fringe of brown mascara.
Last, some powder to set it all,
and color for my lips,
if I can close their wound.

Only one man has seen me do this.
Creation is the most intimate of verities.
Who is entitled to see a woman
form bones where there are none,
or shape a brow?
And who could love me
if they saw my naked eyes?
Men are not fools.

I am afraid for the girls
who refuse the ferocity of artifice.
How else could I have risen
on the morning that you died,
and then were born,
except to make up my face?

Beach

Night is just beneath my skin,
it presses thumbs on my eyes,
its taste on my lips like salt.

The moon has sucked away the shore,
left a pencil line of light
drawn on the rim of breaking water.

The children are running,
crying down the cape like sea birds.
Somewhere in the dark you are running.

Try as I might, I can't see you.
But that flung white might be your arm,
that moonless shape, your face.

The Community of the Deaf

I pray and Sister prays braying,
throat flaming tones unlike any words,
fingers biting into her thumbs.

At the Kiss of Peace I clasp her hand,
a twist of muscle grown powerful
signing the truths:
Woman grows from ribbon, Man from brim.

Body is her body;
one hand lifts the other to form Help.

Jesus is a nail hammered into each palm.
Hope reaches up past the eyes,
Spirit is drawn forth from the mouth.

Joy is an open hand stirring the heart.
Love is fists crossed over the breasts,
shutting all up against the heart.

When motion ceases she is wholly mute.
There is no way to gauge the silence
of a woman who has lost her language.

Ménage à Trois

Taking a thin band of skin
from my ankle,
exposing the white tendon,
he bound a young fox to my leg.

Leashed by my flesh,
the animal howled with pain,
as I did,
when I tried to walk.

I stumbled on his battered paws.
Buffeted under my hobble
he was not too frightened
to bite and tear.

Secretly I made a plan
to cut off my foot
and escape the fox cub.
Better to be crippled but free.

Somehow he guessed.
When I awoke this morning
he had already cut off my foot,
but the fox is still with me.

With a strip of skin
sliced from my thigh
he has roped the fox
between my legs.

I am afraid to make
any more secret plans.
How much must I cut away?

Drawing Up

Timberline, then the last gnarl
and the mountain's scalped,
bone laid bare.

We've climbed to the boulderfield
where thumbnail flowers unclench
for their frantic season.

But I lie down alone on tundra growth.
My feathers fall away.
Exposed at last,
I bend my throat to fix bleached eyes
on the flight of my bones.

There's a white sky over,
a new moon with no voice yet.
You wander on the sullen lichen,
calling,
the mating male who knows
his own insistent cry,
but not my name.

I'm outspread,
plumed and preened to invite
only the blind embrace of light.

Wake

Tonight the dead come visiting,
our black clothes as papery as ash,
as husks.

There are roast meats
and shortbreads on the table,
whiskey and strong tea,
but we aren't hungry.

There's nothing much to say,
even about our suffering.
You hold my chair for me.
The room dries up around us,

who once went under earth
willingly
to eat only the pulpy seeds,
to sleep, rising blind and shadowless,
each following the other
through the single opening
again and again,

who once let our dreams converge
like streams of blood.

Repeated Forms

Snow on stiff dried grass
cracked milkweed pods
filled with ice

ditches run white in last light
no wind in the woodlot

limping hound
ice on his paws
ice on his belly

mother carrying the rabbit
blood on her boot
talking again of a time she almost

the pale field sloping
down toward home

black window squares
mother crying, no smoke!
the gunshot echoing in the barn

The Animal Ship

Even hidden in the ropes I hear
the animals crying
from the hold,

the furious cats, the rage of the bear
with no young to defend
anymore,

the howling apes trying to tear
death from their flesh, birds
broken in crates.

I can smell the sweat of their terror
as we hose their savage dreams
into our wake.

I have been crusted with the despair
of animals, thick as salt
in my clothes.

I taste their suffering in the air.
Gulls refuse our dark decks
pitching below,

afraid to try the drafts of fear
that rise from the ship as all
the animals die.

I want to walk in white rooms, the bare
rooms of my home, their floors
bleached with light.

I want to hear only the clear,
tuneless singing of my mother
at her quiet cares.

Vision

Not yet light, only dim green,
April night still in my bedroom.

Looking out, I see my pale girl
guarding her bitch in mud and moss,

both looking up at the blue looming
goose trapped under clouds and wires,

circling bare crab trees,
shadowless, crying low for Canada.

April

if you husked me tonight
of muddy jeans
and peeled me clean
one long garland down to the core

I'd be revealed
all May Apple, Blue John
Jack-in-the-pulpit

plump with loam and leaf mold
grass pelt, reedy waterfall
through limestone ribs
well water rusty as blood
in every vein

under my fingernails
thin hot slivers of sky
moss spores, humming Jew's harps
on my breath

crack my bones
suck sun for marrow

Missouri Bottomland

I'll be the girl in her daddy's shirt
and her brother's Levi's,
riding in your pickup truck
with the six-pack between my knees,
waiting for the summer day to shut down.

You be the boy in wash pants and white bucks,
smelling of soap and Coke,
driving with one hand.

I've got the army blanket, honey,
you've got the church key,
and after dark the riverbank is blind.

I'll be the girl in the weeds and honeysuckle,
with cool hands and red lollipops,
and a slick, flat belly.

You be the boy who rolls me off the blanket.

I'll be the girl with sand on her bare ass
who makes the stars disappear
with her mouth.

The Lovers

Did you signal to me
as we were drowning?
Your hands said something,
was it my name?
I'd forgotten my name.

Locked into me
in the long dive down
through dark water,
past schools of swimmers
struggling back toward light,
clouds of fish diffusing,
night tides, dulse adrift,
bodies sewn into shrouds.

Primal blackness at the ocean bed,
blind bones,
shells like melon rind,
drifts of sand under my head.

So this is where we began,
so this is where one will begin,
where water is a hopeless weight.

Morning Song

Count down the dawn watch
then switch the sun on
like a lamp.
Let light press out
our damp pillowcase.
Chase me under cover fresh as cream,
lock your legs over me
tight.
Turn the clock face away
and say my morning name
while you're stiff and starched
as new day.

Probably

Probably the child
is yours, but there are no
certainties in summer light.

Perhaps grass, sweat, salt,
green pears, or fear may know how
to impregnate, we can't be sure.

He unfurls alone.
Blindly, with blue slate eyes
and fingers frail as shrimp skin

he creates himself
deeper than you can reach.
I smile at your confusion.

I am swollen
with a lifetime in the grip
of this sea-going stranger

sailing me to land,
and you talk to me of proof.
He exists. The circle is closed.

And if you are not
his father, then the noon heat,
or the deer flies, or another.

On the Ledge

Let sun lay gold
on small old skins.
Take parchments at the splits
where we grew through,
peel up from the feet
sucking sweet filaments
from discarded claws,
cracking shells to grow
new articulations,
darker summer markings.
Under stripped flesh,
fresh amber hairs.

Pull increments of the old dance
over our heads like outgrown leotards,
faded at my nipples,
sticking at your armpits.

Yellowed kid gloves torn off,
colors conjoin, pale and hungry,
on that used twist of us
crumpled into a pillow.

Sleep, dry,
only our white spines left to speak
the shape limits might take.

Wedding

After the elephant act she appears,
caped and veiled in spotlights,
her costume sewn with crystal beads.

He enters in white tights.
His cape is scarlet and his ring shoes, purple.
His bare chest is glossed with sweat.

They are proud and professional,
having practiced this act since birth.
The band is struck up briskly.

Attended by her rose lights
she climbs the rope ladder,
more powerful now than she appeared below.

He climbs the ascent rope,
hand over hand, legs poised,
shoulders laboring in his blue lights.

She rubs her hands with rosin.
Her rhinestone breastplates dazzle.
His rhinestone belt catches all the lights.

They adjust their wrist bands.
They have never been more ready
and their families approve.

Her boyish buttocks tense.
He begins the swing she has awaited,
pumping first for speed, then falling back

until she can catch his rhythm.
The trapeze is silver in her hands;
she slices through the silver lights.

She swings once to check their spacing.
He is smiling, swinging just for her
and waiting for her wrists.

As he passes below her it is time.
She releases her trapeze,
leaping toward his hands, her catcher.

She sees his teeth, his hard belly,
narrow knees flying now above her
as she falls past his reach.

He has caught her feathered head-piece
but they have missed the grip,
and there is no safety net.

Notes on Night-Running

the hour of last lights
massed in upper rooms

through the street lamp warp
woven with rain
I run splashing through yards
wet sandals slapping
a brokenfield flicker
white between fruit trees

my black bitch night wild
devouring dark traces, flushing
hackled secrets from wet grass
keen as glass shards

I break bare-legged
through the hedges after her
needing to peel my painful mind
to the animal core

a wish like the death wish
to be nothing more than headlong running
to be only bonesocket turning

to be only unleashed breath
sucking up musky shadows
from the creekbed street

Anniversary

His eyes have a bruised, oriental lid,
plum-blue with fatigue.
He looks into the nest of his cupped hands,
his nails bitten past the quick,
into flesh.

Did I dream this grave man cherishing
his own mortality,
knowledge that he holds so tenderly,
gently, like a thrush's freckled egg?

And in what milky boyhood dream of his
could he have conceived of me,
my eyes shut tight,
holding back even breath
against the time of no more breath,
both hands clenched,
yolk and white running through my fingers?

Minister Creek

drinking brandy and spying
through the plastic tent
I watch you in the clearing
hanging the pot of apricots
from a cherry branch
out of the reach of racoons

then you're the racoon
sniffing the fruit
searching the creek sand with tiny hands
for crawdads

you're an orange-vermilion lizard
with five fingerprint spots
all tongue and toes
lazing on black bark

you're a woodchuck
squatting on your fat rock
like a smug smile

you're a patent-leather beetle
gray ash on your wings
thrashing on the rim of the fire

you're a white-tailed deer
leaving droppings in the ferns

you're a clear current
cruising among the boulders

you're rejoicing
and you've never learned any words for that

Waiting Room

Almost alone
we sit in the airport
drinking tea with milk,
wide night windows
blurred with steam
seal us in.

My face burns like snow
in your hands.
You thumbprint my eyes, passports.
Refugee from so many embraces,
I've lost the homeland.

Sky is a luminous canopy of silence,
but after I leave
electronic stars
will radio your words to me across the void:
Death means nothing.

Apart from love,
your death means
I will resound
without relief
to the signals of my own.

Breaking Out

Under broken bark
skin burns.
Words flicker to ash,
logs groan in the grate
like bodies spent and rolling away.

I see your fat mouth flash,
your grin splits you end to end.
You steam and shriek sap.

Every door we open
breaks into flame in our hands,
crumbles into the roar.

Our babies have left their cots,
their covers lift and quiver in the blaze,
their clothes shrivel like leaves.

The hallway is a throat crazed with fire,
and I'm the cracked and blackened tongue
shaping cries.
But who remembers my name
and is searching?

Alice in Wonderland

I wonder if I am a monster to you
as the man seemed to me
who loved me more and more
and would not be stopped
could not be contained
or held in check
by threats or promises
who grew and grew
in size and weight
his flesh as dense as earth
his dreams as dense as flesh
when already I was shrinking
back into myself
holding my self
the small kernels in my hands
closing my fists
and hiding in my hands

I was afraid of him
a gigantic frog prince
who came into my dreams
a paratrooper into the walled city
a guerrilla
a gypsy from the alley

And now I'm the one
disordered and unkempt
outgrowing everything already
pregnant with longing
ranging out of chairs
overflowing the bed
bumping into doorways
Are you afraid now?

You prize restraint
and I am vast and barely covered
by my skin
even my hands are swollen
and clumsy
and topple you when I mean to touch
Will you crouch and dodge desire
as I did?

Twins

The two of us in one belly.
Passion, that fat mother
floating us, feeding us,
absorbing blows.

We twisted in our small space,
drinking the same salty fluid,
fed with the same blood, blind.

Light and dark like our limbs twining.
All those fingers, ours—
four hands for the two of us.
The one membrane for both.

The way out like a way in,
blank and fiery, skulls crushing,
air lacerating our lungs,
faces as in weeping.
And the surgical necessities, after.

Late at night when my skin aches
where your skin was sliced away,
when my bones hurt
where your bones were broken away,

I want back in.

The Sacrament of Penance

For gar-fishing,
take a lantern
and troll the deep, broken, black
Ozark lake,
where drowned pin oaks reach up,
brushing your prow.

Gar rise blind
from blind depths,
muscle without minds,
only eyes sighting lamps for prey.

If you want blood instead of meat,
wait on that black gauze,
and when their blank gaze
flashes,
smash down with a gaff
or an oar.

Like me, you'll pull out flesh
to fling into the bilge
of your rented boat.

Part Two: Holy Women

". . . those women . . . had found the means for Being *within themselves* . . . and they could not suppress this, when they came among people, but shimmered as though they consorted always with the blessed. Who can say how many they were, or who they were. It is as if they had destroyed beforehand the words with which one might grasp them."

Rainer Maria Rilke, *The Notebooks of Malte Laurids Brigge*

Considerations on
Indo-European Culture

the words for salmon
for birch tree
for willow
for wolf and bear
assure us that you were

women whom I remember
without any words at all

small and seldom-smiling
black hair braided

walking in the long grass
calling the wolves to your side

carrying on your hips
clinging bear babies
leaping salmon babies
giving them milkweed pods
to suck on

cooking in the smoky hut
birch cloth wrapped around
tucked in
arms out-stretched unadorned

drinking honey beer with bread

lying down in the tawny dusk
salmon babies at the breast
bear babies at the breast
warm belly beds
for all the naked babies

nothing but skin between you
and all your skin the same skin
all smoky all downy all brown

all your words the same words
for birch and salmon and bear

Christine de Pisan

I dreamed the shape of the universe,
bivalved as an oyster
shutting itself softly
onto its precise shadowless edge,
like lips closing in death.

It is like my cupped hands
which I close over that empty space
in which I exist,
over darkness.
No other hand fits mine in this way.
The rims of Heaven and Hell meet
and rest without warp.

I can hold the one half in my circling arm
as I hold my child,
and embrace the other half
as I hold my lover.

Oval.
But where my hands join
they are burned and raw with this truth.

The Poetress Li Chi'ng Chao

Small and pliant sister,
holding your silver mirror in your cupped hands,
an offering,

an image of the ecstasy
that stripped your skin
like a silk garment,
leaving flesh so wakeful
a plum blossom burned.

Gauze bit your supple arms
with its pale burden.

Even a random smile,
snuffling after your secret poise,
was too much to bear
for one who took up anguish
simply, like a gift,
as we accept our reflections
as our selves.

Nothing compensated, when he had gone,
nothing satisfied, or else you were sated
on a sip of wine
or a crisp, single shoot.

You bound your breasts down,
your hair you fashioned
into a black chrysanthemum,
crying when your sleeves fell back
revealing unbruised skin.

But seated at your dressing table
you out-distanced all your comforters.

Fearlessly alone
you crept into the chrysalis
of your purple blanket
and waited for the white rim of morning
to rise on the wind screens.

Your fingers rustled into a nest for your cheek.

Archeologist

The cellar crouches on its haunches.
Its stone spine cuts a channel in clay,
but goldenrod has broken the bricks,
saplings have pierced tiles,
wild grass holds the space at bay.

I'm here to see my trench,
this kiva shaped to an ancient order,
cloistered and severe,
how passages, root rooms, coal chutes
still stink with a dark sap
that sticks like pitch or blood,
smells like bitter, homemade beer.

I've come back to camp in the tiger pit,
to live without rooms or roof.
I can sleep between the sky and the stone
and dig until I find that charred word
rare as a bronze bead: No.
It was the one thing of my own.

Gaspara Stampa

I am the giantess
pressed against the inside of the earth
like a snail clinging inside a fishbowl,

my breasts and belly curving up
under the bulge of continents.
I look out through the broken eyes
of the mountains.

Under the crust
the world reverses, as in a mirror.
I push through the pulp of rock
like a whale trapped under polar ice.

I taste the deepest salt
and spread my arms and legs
to lie tight up under the sea floor,
as beneath a lover,
sky refracted through a thousand years
of drifting shells.

At the equator
I strain through coral doors,
emerging into the weight of stars,
to float, an island in the moonless night.

Banners of constellations describe
their perfect parabola, East to West.
I point my feet
towards the edge where the red flares set,

but there is no way home.

The Hired Mourner

I held an edge
of the crimson tissue canopy,
and tied on a white silk shawl.

I tore my hair
and rubbed my arms with ashes.
I bound hemp cords against my skin.

I followed you down the path
between old graves adorned
with paper flags for soldiers,
with dolls dressed in the garments
of dead infants.

Your rigid limbs wrapped in linen,
they laid you down
and piled up dirt and stones.

I recited the prayers
and burned sandalwood incense
and drank rice wine from blue cups.

I had brought an apple for your grave,
but, Little Mother,
when the others had gone back,
I sat down in the sun,
dizzy with wine,
and ate that fruit myself.

Before I left you,
I gathered up my robes in both hands,
the way you taught your daughters,
and pissed behind the mulberry bushes.

Mrs. Nakamura

Imprinted on stone,
delicate skeleton,
prehistoric fish
holding her straw broom,
head bowed,
six hundred yards from the center
of the blast.

Scientists may examine
a woman fossilized
while attending to her sweeping
in the instant before she glanced up
at the exploding god.

The Elephant Goddess

I am old and thin as bamboo.
I have no breasts.
I wear my flowered sarong
but I have no shoes now
since our temples have been destroyed.

The elephants still know me.
I put my arms around their trunks
and hold them as they rock and moan.

The jungle crouches around us.
As we gather under the stone lanterns
snakes draw back from our circle.

I tell of when their prayers were young
and pungent with incense,
of when I danced the prayer dance
in slippers of red and silver,

of when elephants fathered my children,
sun child, moon child, rain child,
my breasts full of milk for all of them.

The night is white with the moon gaze
but I will not dance now.
I have put off the garments of silk,
the jewels, the khol,
the old costumes of illusion and desire.

I have rubbed myself with ashes
and put on the skin of elephants,
the mask and tusks of elephants.

I will bury their bones and ivory tonight
in the place of the holiest of bones.

Sappho

Like a Brujo's lizard
you began with your lips sewn shut,
as though a lover's teeth
were biting you to silence.

Your language was the knives
and flames of your hands,
knees speaking like mountain creeks
cutting through stone
with their slender voices,
your breasts soft mutterings,
soft murmurs between your thighs,
gasps at your armpits.

The sweet swamp was receding,
seed pods blowing,
tongues of reeds waiting
as you lay back on the shallow sea,
circling in the green currents
like a ship of sighs,
watching clouds form and reform
into the shapes of your unspoken dreams.

Then a gentle unraveler
pressed her fingers between your lips
and your clear cries
burst from your throat
like deep sea divers ravenous for air.

Cleis. Dica. Atthis. Anactoria.
Eros.
Aphrodite! Aphrodite!

Georgia O'Keefe

A woman with almost the body of a man
lives in her adobe facing West.

Only what she needs is with her,
her bowl and blue pot,
her bench, roped bed,
her white calf's skull.

Mornings, she weeds squash and beans.
After the blank noon heat
she paints the shapes ironed
onto her mind's hot horizon.

When the desert night comes on suddenly,
that silent metaphor,
she leaves her lamp unlit
and lies down on the earth,
letting the sand press her upwards,
knowing her own unfurling
against the unfurling dark.

Muse

He dove into her as into the sea,
feeling her give under him
as he sank into her broken shadow.
He called her Lady of the Gleam of the Sea.

He felt her as element around him,
without horizon,
bearing him up, drawing him on as a tide.

He said, the gleam of the moon's eyelids
of the lady of the golden necklace
will bring harm both to me and to her.

But he floated.

She grew vaster in each adulation,
she drowned whole islands,
she rose and fell with the moon,
but still he would not stop.

She closed the hawk-moon of her eyes
and dreamed of making bread,
of folding linen,
but he sang on,
drifting always out from her shore.

The Liberian Whore

The instructions have always been:
be a still pond with clear water,
a place of rest.

Arrange my hair in flower shapes
so that he might unfurl blossoms,
wear many underskirts
so he might draw them aside
one by one.
Polish my skin with oils.

Be new
every time.

I welcome him when he comes to my room.
I tell him my name, Noemi.
He calls me Little Bird.

He wears bracelets, as if to a feast.
His tongue is thick with his desire.

He sits by me on my mat.
I give him seeds seasoned with spice,
mangoes that I cut in my lap,
and feed him from my hand.
I sing for him the only song,
and he lies back, waiting.

I am the small, soft creature
into whom he will disappear,
utterly.

I am the delicate bird
who flies into his mouth,
tearing down through his lungs
to beat my bloody wings
inside his bowels.

Astride his body I ride him out to sea,
my hair stiff with sweat and semen,
my hands buried in his flesh and my own.

My eyes are scraped clean and aching
in the brine.
I am stretched into a bowsprit.
He will drown under his vessel.
My legs will tear him to pieces.

I am the raging shark going through bone
after the heart,
eating myself alive.

Chinese Burial Cloth,
Second Century

You wrapped it around yourself,
Grandmother Ch'ang,
and lay down in its silk.

It is printed in the pattern
you made for your weaver.
The golden cherry boughs are Love.
The crimson hawks are Passion,
and their green talons, Truth.
The blood-brown stains on the throat
and hems are Hope.

Your gown is your daughter,
speaking of you, telling of your life.
You outlived them all,
those others who did not bleed
through their bandages.

Recital

She stands unadorned,
we lean toward her, ready.

Then broken, atonal, severe,
like an eye of stone
gazing without flickering

we know the oldest song,
of the first hands touching,
of the one who never returns.

Song heard through water,
of heartbeats magnified to thunder
in another.

Song that we smear on our breasts
like honey, like milk,
song that tastes of salt.

The singer is resonant in her silence.
Her hands tremble,
but she does not sing.

After a while we go away,
one by one, each one alone,
having heard.

Loving the White Bull

The disguise made for me
was of white woven silk,
eyes huge and amber,
hooves polished jewels,
ears tufted with milkweed floss.

I crept into it eagerly,
curved my back up into the spine,
pushed my head into the skull
ornamented with the delicate crown of horns.

Radiant creature, I could raise my tail up
like a braided silken whip!

Wheeled to his pen,
I called him Moon Bull,
God Gift,
Sire of the Firmament,
Mystery!

Scenting me
he crashed the gate,
his teeth cracked my shoulders,
his weight tore flesh,
blood ran down between my thighs.

Flecked with red, he rampaged,
battering his blind head
against the fences,
trampling both costume and desire
into the mire.

Metchilde

Metchilde
flaming like a charcoal grill
toasted her sweetmeats of love
until they roused the appetite
not only of the Holy Spirit
but of the animals of the wood

they stormed the convent
the unicorn white raw silk
his tongue tinged with blood

the lion his genitals as red
as torn flesh with love

the tawny dogs
the hunting cats
clambering toward her like waves of wheat
against a thresher

and all the wild horses
plunging and snorting
and all the nameless beasts
too dark too dear to name

to Metchilde gentle cook
her flesh unfolding like a rose exploding

watching only the One
not all these lesser ones
roiling in her courtyard
leaving their droppings on the flagstones

burning her flesh in her cell
burning her heart at her prie-dieu
smiling with vague gaiety
because her leaping heart was already gone

and the animals impaling themselves
on the gate posts
on the iron fence
tearing out their bowels with desire
below her unlighted window

Drawing Her Again

The spine of the graffiti goddess
bleeds down the wall,
a spray-can smear of red,
the last breath bent under,
as if a woman's tailbone was necessary, too,

as if the circle breasts,
nipple blasts,
the forked vulva with its long slit
haven't revealed enough
to those of us waiting for the train.

Primitive: a torso,
head an empty cup shape
with open lips floating in it.

Others are watching,
but I find my marking pen,
stretch to draw the arc of her skull,
snake twist of hair,
two Etruscan eyes.

Working quickly now—
the train whistle blowing—
I give her arms, hands, legs,
finish her feet just off the floor.
Six feet tall, easily.

The men in raincoats don't smile,
but I do,
seeing her completed,
staring straight through me,
through these others,
concrete behind her unlidded eyes.